Newgrange Press

Let Me Decide

Dr. D. William Molloy
MB, Bch, BAO, MRCP(I), FRCP(C)

William was born in Waterford, Ireland, and qualified in medicine in 1977, at University College, Cork. He came to Canada in 1981 and trained in Geriatrics at the University of Manitoba, University of Western Ontario, and McMaster University.

A consultant geriatrician, he is currently director of the Memory Clinic and the Geriatric Research Group at the Hamilton Civic Hospitals. A Professor of Medicine at McMaster University he has authored and co-authored, *Vital Choices; What Are We Going To Do Now; Capacity To Decide; Alzheimer Disease; The Fine Detail; SMMSE: A User's Guide; Dysfunctional Behavior In Dementia; and Let Me Pass Gently.* He is married to Deborah and they have two sons, James and Alexander.

Let Me Decide

The Health and Personal Care Directive That Speaks for You When You Can't...

Dr. William Molloy
MB, FRCP(C)

First published December 1989
Second edition published November 1990
Third edition published June 1992
Fourth edition published April 1996
Fifth edition published July 1998
Sixth edition published May 2000

ISBN 0-9694645-6-8

1. Terminally ill – Medical Care
2. Terminally ill – Living Will
3. Patient Advocacy

Published in 2000 by Newgrange Press

Newgrange Press (Canada), Orkney House, 440 Orkney Road, RR 1, Troy, Ontario L0R 2B0, Canada
Telephone: (905) 628-0354, Fax: (905) 628-4901 Email: idecide@netcom.ca

Newgrange Press (USA), 302 Highland Avenue, Winchester, Mass 01890 USA
Telephone/Fax: 781.729.8981 Email: jamesmcinerny@hotmail.com

Newgrange Press (Ireland), The Stables, Woodstown, Waterford, Ireland
Telephone: 353-51-870152, Fax: 353-51-871214

Newgrange Press (Australia), Box 7077, Shenton Park, 6008 Western Australia, Australia
Telephone: 61-8-93896433, Fax: 61-8-93896455

Newgrange Press (Japan), 100-1, Kashiyama, Habikino, Osaka, (583-0886), Japan
Telephone: 81-729-542000. Fax: 81-729-547560

Newgrange Press (Austria), Willersdorferstrasse 6, A-8601 St. Radegund, Austria
Telephone: 0043.3132.3472, Fax: 0043.3132.3472.15

Visit the Let Me Decide website at: www.newgrangepress.com

Printed in Canada

This book is dedicated to Alexander

*When making your choice in life,
do not forget to live.*

Dr. Samuel Johnson

Contents

Let
Me
Decide

1

Introduction

The purpose of this booklet is to help you take control of – and help you to record your wishes for – your health and personal care, if you were unable to speak for yourself. If at some time in the future you become incapacitated by disease or injury and cannot communicate for yourself, the "Let Me Decide" Health and Personal Care Directive will speak for you. It is your Living Will.

Over the last fifty years, medicine has advanced at an amazing pace. What would have been considered miraculous in the 1920s or '30s is now routine. People are kept alive with heart, kidney and liver transplants. Arms are sewn back on, and cancers that were once fatal are cured. At the same time, modern medicine has become more technological, more sophisticated and more complicated.

The general public can be overwhelmed by the amount of technology used in providing modern health care. People are confused by the jargon that health professionals use. A person can go into hospital and have an ECG, EEG, EMG, colonoscopy, laparoscopy, bronchoscopy or a hundred other tests for diseases such as SLE, COPD, or IHD. The person with a disease experiences pain, shortness of breath, weight loss or tiredness; this jargon is meaningless. Blood tests and x-rays mean more needles and scans to create endless printouts and images on screens. The discussions and decisions about tests and treatments can be overwhelming.

At the same time, through newspapers, magazines, television and films, the general public has become better educated about illnesses and treatments. Groups such as Alzheimer Society, Cystic Fibrosis Foundation, Cancer Society and Kidney Foundation also provide information and support. More and more, patients and their families want to retain control over their medical procedures and health care. At the same time, they feel helpless in the face of modern technology. This combination of high technology and better informed patients can lead to conflict between patients, their families and the health care team. Large, modern hospitals have become vast medical-industrial complexes that sometimes overwhelm and bewilder patients.

Medical staff face an additional dilemma. Doctors don't want to take responsibility for decisions that will affect the rest of a patient's life. But without guidance from the patient, doctors are obliged to follow the hospital policies, and procedures demand that they must do everything to preserve life.

The freedom to decide one's own destiny is the right of every competent person. This includes the right to accept or refuse treatments. Many people want to choose their own health care because they have definite opinions on how they want to be treated. But if we become critically ill, we may not be able to make these decisions. For example, people with pneumonia or those who have suffered a stroke may be too confused to make their wishes known.

Many are concerned that in the event of a serious illness they may not receive the treatment they would want. They worry that they may become too sick to let doctors know their wishes, or that they may not even be asked. Some fear that they will be connected to machines and kept alive despite a very poor quality of life. These treatments may just drag out the dying process and prolong their suffering. They fear they will be kept alive in a condition they would find intolerable because of suffering, loss of dignity, without freedom or independence. Some fear dying more than death. Intolerable conditions are considered "states worse than death."

If you become ill or confused, family, friends or doctors are put in a position where they must make decisions for you. These decisions are often very difficult; they can present a "no-win" situation for everyone.

If members of a family ask the doctors to do "everything" to keep a loved one alive and that person dies in a few weeks or months, the family may feel guilty that they put the patient through needless tests and treatments. They may feel that treatment only prolonged the patient's suffering and postponed his or her death. On the other hand, if they let their family member "die with dignity," they may feel later that they should have done more.

Problems develop if the family members cannot agree. Some may want "everything" done to keep the person alive at all costs. Others may want palliative care for comfort and relief of pain. Further complications can arise when children from divorced marriages resent step-parents or common-law spouses making decisions for their parents. Children who have been out of contact for many years can turn up when a parent is dying, and try to involve themselves in the decisions. These children may demand that doctors do "everything" to try to bring the parent back. They feel guilty and want to make peace with the parent. Friends and other family members who remained in close contact are more likely to accept the parent's death more easily, and request only palliative care. Family conflicts and disagreements can leave lasting bitterness and resentment.

How can we protect ourselves to make sure we get the health care we want? How can we let others know our wishes? How can we protect our families and friends from this dilemma?

Discussing these issues in advance can prevent conflict later. But the drawback of informal discussions about these matters is that family and friends may not recall them accurately. Perhaps years later, in a time of crisis, the family tries to interpret what the person said and meant.

If we have stated our wishes clearly, doctors and family don't have to second-guess what kind of treatment we would want. Clear instructions prevent conflict and guilt in the family, removing the need for "second-guessing." If you leave clear instructions for your health and personal care, then if the time comes when you are too sick to decide for yourself, your doctors, family and friends will know your wishes. You will receive the treatment you want. You take your family "off the hook."

2

What Is an Advance Directive?

An *advance directive* is a written statement that expresses a person's wishes in advance.

The most widely used advance directive is your *will*. It contains specific instructions—directives—about your possessions. Your *will* informs others how you want your possessions distributed after your death.

A different kind of advance directive is a *power of attorney*. This directive empowers another person (a substitute, proxy or mandatory) to act on your behalf if you ever become unable to make decisions yourself.

An advance directive that deals specifically with health care is called a *living will*, or Health Care Directive. It contains instructions about your care in case you are not able to make health care decisions at a later date. The "Let Me Decide" Health and Personal Care Directive (Living Will) enables you to state your wishes for medical treatment and personal care.

As long as you remain competent, able to consider and communicate health care choices, you must make these decisions for yourself. **An advance directive is only used if you are incompetent and unable to make your wishes known.**

There are two types of Health Care Directives– "instructional" and "proxy."

INSTRUCTIONAL DIRECTIVE

An *instructional directive* states which treatments are wanted or not wanted under any given circumstance. These statements can be general or specific. The more specific the instructions, the easier it will be for family and doctors to follow.

An instructional directive is not limited to the treatment of terminal or irreversible conditions—it can also apply to curable, reversible conditions.

PROXY DIRECTIVE

A *proxy directive* nominates a substitute (power

of attorney or proxy) to make decisions for your health or personal care if you become incompetent. This substitute has the ability to make health and personal care decisions in much the same way as a financial power of attorney can manage our finances.

POWER OF ATTORNEY
FOR PERSONAL CARE

The "Let Me Decide" Health and Personal Care Directive has both an *instructional* and *proxy directive*. This provides double reinforcement that your wishes are followed. For example, if the written instructions are not specific enough to guide a doctor in a particular situation, the substitute can provide more input. If the substitute is not available during a crisis, the written instructions will inform the doctor of your wishes.

3

Is an Advance Directive Legal?

Court cases have established the rights of people to complete advance directives. Organizations such as the Canadian Medical Association have recommended and supported advance directives as the best way to deal with decision-making in the care of people who are incompetent.

Some provinces recognize proxy directives, others recognize both proxy and instructional directives. Your "Let Me Decide" Directive allows you to name a substitute (proxy, power of attorney for personal care, mandatory) and give clear instructions at the same time.

It is important that you select someone upon whom you can rely and who is likely to be available to carry out your wishes. You can also name an alternative as a backup if the substitute is not available. You need to discuss your wishes for health and personal care with the person you appoint as your substitute.

When you are satisfied that this individual understands what you want and can carry out your wishes, leave written instructions with that substitute. This person is then bound to follow your instructions unless and until there is excellent reason to believe circumstances would have caused you to change your mind.

An Advance Directive is a legally binding document in British Columbia, Manitoba, Ontario, Quebec and Nova Scotia.

It is now legal to appoint a *substitute* (called a substitute decision-maker) in British Columbia, a *power of attorney for personal care* in Ontario, a *mandatory* in Quebec, or a *proxy* in Manitoba to make personal and health care decisions on behalf of a patient or client.

BRITISH COLUMBIA

In British Columbia, an Advance Directive can include health and personal care matters. The laws allow people to name a substitute decision-maker to make health care, personal care, legal and financial decisions for them. The laws also allow people to make detailed instructions about these matters.

MANITOBA

In 1993, Manitoba legislated the right of persons 16 or older to complete a Health Care Directive and name a proxy. No special form is required. The Health Care Directive must only be signed and dated. The form does not need to be witnessed. The proxy must be at least 18 years old.

NOVA SCOTIA

In Nova Scotia, legislation allows a competent adult to name a substitute. The substitute acts on an individual's behalf if that person becomes incapable of making decisions.

ONTARIO

Legislation in Ontario allows a person, 16 or older, to assign another person power of attorney for personal care. The power of attorney form can also contain instructions about the person's specific wishes. The substitute may not be anyone providing health care services to the client for pay. There are certain requirements for it to be valid: two witnesses, 18 or older, neither related to, nor associated with the substitute, are required. The witnesses must believe the client is competent at the time. The directions contained in the power of attorney must always be taken into consideration by those providing for the care of the client.

QUEBEC

In Quebec, a person appoints a substitute by preparing a mandate in advance of incapacity. The substitute (or mandatory) can act on behalf of the client when that client, at a later date, becomes incompetent. The mandate is made in the presence of two witnesses who are required to attest to the client's capacity at the time it is signed. The mandate cannot be put into effect until a court has confirmed the incompetence of the client. Quebec has not specified any special form as a mandate.

ALBERTA, NEW BRUNSWICK, NEWFOUNDLAND, PRINCE EDWARD ISLAND, SASKATCHEWAN, AND THE TERRITORIES

In these provinces, and in the territories, there is no current legislation governing advance directives. However, clear instructions (such as directives) about your health care would, we hope, be honoured.

4

The "Let Me Decide" Directive: An Overview

The "Let Me Decide" Directive, or Living Will, can be used by adults of all ages to plan their future health and personal care.

The Directive uses medical terms so that doctors and families can interpret it clearly. If you want to use the "Let Me Decide" Directive, you must learn what these terms mean. To help you, a glossary is included at the back of this booklet. For more information, you should consult your family doctor.

The Directive provides a variety of treatment options, depending on whether your condition is acceptable or irreversible/intolerable. You can choose a level of medical treatment or care for a life threatening illness, for feeding problems or if your heart stops (cardiac arrest).

The "Let Me Decide" Personal Health Care Directive has five sections. The purpose of each section is explained below.

1. INTRODUCTION

This section states the reasons why you want to complete this Directive. It advises others that the Directive should not be used while you are conscious and capable of making decisions for yourself. It should only be used if you are incapacitated by disease or injury and unable to make your own decisions. It revokes any previous documents and establishes this document as the latest expression of your wishes. In this section, your substitute (power of attorney, proxy, mandatory) is named.

2. PERSONAL STATEMENT

This section contains your personal statement, which can be used to cover any particular area of health or personal care that is not covered in the other parts of the Directive. You can use this statement to make individual choices.

It has an introductory phrase: *"I consider an irreversible/intolerable condition to be any condition..."* Complete this in your own words to tell others what level of disability you would consider unacceptable or intolerable.

Most people would want different care depending on whether they were in a acceptable or irreversible/intolerable condition. Try to state your wishes as clearly as possible.

In your personal statement you can also state your wishes regarding personal care issues such as where you live, safety issues, clothing and hygiene. In this section you can also make your wishes known about organ donation, blood transfusion, post mortem and cremation.

3. HEALTH CARE CHART

This chart documents your wishes for treatment of life-threatening illness, cardiac arrest and feeding. Different choices are available depending on whether your condition is acceptable or irreversible/intolerable.

We recommend that you and your doctor review your instructions in the chart every year or so. Space is provided for this updated information. If you review it and plan to make no changes, just write "no change," sign and date it with your doctor. But if you want to change your wishes, you must tell your substitutes and family doctor. Update all the copies of the directive and have everybody sign them.

4. DEFINITIONS

This section contains a brief explanation of terms used in the Directive.

You will not automatically receive your chosen level of care for every illness. For example, if you asked for "intensive care" for a life-threatening illness, you would not automatically be admitted to intensive care every time you became ill. If admitted to hospital with a bleeding ulcer, for example, you might not necessarily require intensive care. Intensive care will only be provided if indicated and if beds are available.

On the other hand, if you requested "palliative care" for an illness, you might have surgery. For example, if you broke your hip and had severe pain, surgery might be the only way to relieve your pain. In this case you could require surgery to put a pin and plate in the bone to fix the hip and relieve the pain. In this case surgery is performed to relieve suffering and keep you comfortable.

5. SIGNATURES (Family Doctor, Substitutes and Witnesses)

In this section, the names, addresses and telephone numbers of your family doctor, substitutes (proxy, power of attorney for personal care, mandatory) and witnesses are provided. Home and work numbers should be given, along with additional numbers where these people can be reached in an emergency.

Witnesses are not required in Manitoba. In Ontario witnesses can be anyone *except* the following:

- the spouse or child (natural or adopted) of the person completing the Directive
- the substitute
- the substitute's spouse or child (natural or adopted)
- any agent of the facility in which the person is completing the Directive is residing
- any business associate of the person who is completing the Directive
- anyone who will inherit money or property from the person who is completing the Directive
- anyone who is less than 18 years old

In Ontario, witnesses are not required to assess the capacity of the person to understand the implications of his or her choices. In Quebec the witnesses must attest to the person's capacity when the mandate is signed.

Now first let's consider what we mean by "acceptable" and "irreversible/intolerable." Life-threatening illnesses, feeding and cardiac arrest are discussed in later chapters.

5

Irreversible/Intolerable and Acceptable Conditions

IRREVERSIBLE AND INTOLERABLE CONDITIONS

When your condition is irreversible/ intolerable, there is no possibility of a complete recovery. Illnesses such as Alzheimer's disease, Parkinson's disease, certain cancers, strokes and AIDS are examples of irreversible/intolerable illnesses that will probably lead to permanent disability and leave you with a poor quality of life.

People react differently depending on their disability. Some people would not consider themselves disabled if they were confined to a wheelchair of even bedridden. Others would consider this an unacceptable loss of independence.

For instance, if Beethoven had gone blind instead of deaf, he still could have heard his music. Blindness would have made little difference to him. But a painter like Picasso would dread blindness much more than deafness. So in this way, the same disabilities can affect people in very different ways.

Since each person would accept different irreversible disabilities, it's important to know in advance what you would not be prepared to accept. Otherwise, your family and doctor may have to guess what you would have wanted. Before you fill out the "Let Me Decide" Directive, you need to think about what level of care you would want with an irreversible disability. Consider this carefully and discuss it with your substitutes and doctor.

Diseases such as cancer, multiple sclerosis, stroke, Parkinson's or Alzheimer's may affect your ability to think and function independently. But don't think in terms of specific illnesses. Instead, consider how these illnesses could impair your independence and freedom or your ability to carry out everyday activities such as walking, dressing, talking and eating. Consider how that would affect your quality of life. Think of what condition you would not be prepared to accept when you define an "irreversible/ intolerable condition" in your Personal Statement.

ACCEPTABLE CONDITION

If you are in an acceptable condition, you may still have a good quality of life. If you had a good quality of life and developed a life-threatening illness such as a bleeding ulcer or pneumonia that could be cured with treatment, without any permanent disability, how would you want to be treated?

If you had a good quality of life in a reversible/acceptable condition, your instructions for the treatment of a life-threatening illness may permit the use of technologies that you would not want in an irreversible/intolerable state. For example, you might want antibiotics for pneumonia if you were otherwise fit and healthy. You might reject antibiotics if you developed pneumonia when you had terminal cancer (irreversible/intolerable condition) which had spread all over your body and was incurable.

Consider which conditions you consider acceptable and irreversible/intolerable, and what level of care you would want in each case.

6

Life-Threatening Illness

The "Let Me Decide" Health and Personal Care Directive enables you to state the level of care you would want in the event of life-threatening illness. You may choose different levels of care if your condition is acceptable or irreversible/ intolerable.

A life-threatening illness can cause death. Pneumonia or bleeding ulcers are examples of life-threatening illnesses. Although pneumonia can be fatal, most healthy people recover fully from it with appropriate treatment. A healthy child or adult who develops pneumonia would want to be vigorously treated. Patients with chronic illnesses may be so weak that they have no resistance to fight the pneumonia. A person who is already dying from in incurable illness may wish to allow the pneumonia to run its course. In this condition a person might not want antibiotics. Palliative care may be appropriate to relieve suffering and maintain comfort.

People with chronic illnesses such as Parkinson's disease, Alzheimer's or cancer often die from the complications of these diseases, such as from pneumonia or blood clots to the lungs (pulmonary embolism).

If a decision is made to treat an acute life-threatening illness in a dying patient, more tests and investigations may be required. This means more needles, x-rays, intravenous lines or even surgery. These procedures can be uncomfortable and painful for the patient. Treatment may only serve to prolong the dying process.

Doctors may advise families in these cases to allow the person to die peacefully, to prevent the patient from suffering any further. Palliative care aims to keep the person comfortable and relieve pain. The goal is not cure, but comfort and relief from suffering.

For this reason, pneumonia has sometimes been called "an old man's friend." It allows a dying person to die peacefully, without a great deal of suffering. You can choose from four levels of care: palliative, limited, surgical, and intensive for the treatment of any life-threatening illness.

PALLIATIVE CARE

At this level, tests and treatments are done, not to prolong life, but to maintain comfort. The aim of treatment is to relieve pain and keep the patient warm, dry and as pain-free as possible.

Patients who have requested this level of care might have surgery, if that could improve their comfort or relieve pain. For example, if you broke a hip and had requested palliative care, surgery could be performed to pin the hip, if this was the most effective way to relieve the pain.

Similarly, antibiotics might be prescribed, not to cure an infection, but because they might improve your comfort.

If you requested palliative care and had bleeding in the stomach or intestine, you would not receive blood transfusions or drugs to stop the bleeding. If you were at home, you would not be transferred to hospital for tests or treatments unless you could not be kept comfortable in your home.

LIMITED CARE

This level includes more treatment than "palliative," but less than "surgical." For example, if you wanted limited care and developed pneumonia, you could receive antibiotics, blood tests, intravenous fluids, x-rays and oxygen. If you had bleeding from the stomach or intestine, you could receive blood transfusions and drugs to stop the bleeding.

You would not receive emergency surgery to stop the bleeding or medical tests that required a general anaesthetic. You would not be put on life-support machines. You would not go on a kidney machine (for dialysis) if your kidneys failed. If you were at home when you became ill, you could be transferred to hospital if enough care could not be provided in the home.

SURGICAL CARE

At this level you would receive blood tests, x-rays, surgery, and be put on a kidney machine if necessary. You would be put on a breathing machine (a ventilator) during or after surgery if necessary. Some people need ventilators for a short time after surgery until they are able to breathe on their own again. You would receive intravenous fluids and blood transfusions if you had life-threatening bleeding from the bowel. A tube might be passed into the bowel (endoscopy) to find the cause of bleeding. If necessary, doctors would perform surgery to correct the bleeding.

You would not be transferred to intensive care, unless that was necessary to keep you comfortable. You would be transferred from home to hospital, without hesitation, for surgical care.

INTENSIVE CARE

At this level, everything a modern hospital has to offer would be used to maintain your life. You would receive surgery, biopsies and life-support systems (kidney machines, breathing machines). Some patients might receive transplant surgery if necessary (including heart, kidney, liver or bone-marrow transplants). If you were at home, you would be transferred to hospital. If you were in a small community hospital, you could be transferred to a larger hospital for a wider range of diagnostic tests and treatments.

7

Feeding

Many people with severe illnesses are not able to feed themselves. Someone must decide if and how they will be fed. If they are unconscious and can't swallow or communicate, they must receive fluids or food artificially to stay alive.

The "Let Me Decide" Directive lets others know your wishes about the kind of feeding you would want if you were not able to feed yourself. There are four ways to feed people who are not able to feed themselves: basic, supplemental, intravenous and tube.

BASIC FEEDING

At this level of care you would be spoon-fed with a regular diet (fluid and solids). You would receive fluids, if you were uncomfortable from thirst. For people who are conscious, dehydration can be very uncomfortable. If you could not swallow, you might require subcutaneous (under the skin) or intravenous fluids to prevent dehydration. The amount of fluid given to prevent dehydration is much smaller than the amount required for feeding through an intravenous line. At the basic level, intravenous fluids can be given, but they are given for comfort, not for feeding.

SUPPLEMENTAL FEEDING
(includes basic feeding)

At this level, supplements are given in addition to a basic diet. For instance, you may be able to swallow solids, but not liquids, or vice versa. If you were not able to eat a regular diet, you would be given high-energy supplements or vitamins. This level does not include tubes or intravenous feeding.

INTRAVENOUS FEEDING
(includes supplemental feeding)

At this level, fluids and food can be given directly into the veins. This method only works for a limited time because the needles required for intravenous feeding eventually damage the veins. When the veins in the arms can no longer be used, larger veins nearer the heart, or in the chest and neck, are used. Through these larger veins, it's possible to give more food and fluids directly into the circulation. This method of feeding is called "total parenteral nutrition."

Intravenous feeding is used for people whose intestines are not absorbing food. If this occurs, there is no point giving special diets by mouth or into the stomach. In this case only intravenous feeding can sustain life.

Intravenous feeding does not require major surgery. Intravenous lines can be inserted into the large veins near the heart, using minor procedures under local anaesthetic.

TUBE FEEDING
(includes intravenous feeding)

Tube feeding includes nasogastric and/or gastrostomy tubes. Nasogastric tubes are soft plastic tubes passed through the nose into the stomach. They are used for people who can digest food but can't swallow. Most people tolerate them well, but some people find them uncomfortable and tend to pull them out again and again.

Gastrostomy tubes are passed through the skin, directly into the stomach. This method of feeding is used for people who can't swallow or can't tolerate a nasogastric tube. When a person needs feeding for a long time, this method is preferable to a nasogastric tube.

Gastrostomy tubes can be surgically installed without a general anaesthetic. Once they are in place, they are fairly painless and trouble-free. People can even have baths and showers with them. They can be used to give people enough food and fluids to sustain them indefinitely.

8

Cardio-Pulmonary Resuscitation

Cardio-pulmonary resuscitation (CPR) is an emergency procedure that attempts to restore breathing and heartbeat in a person whose heart or breathing, or both, have stopped. Because it is an emergency when the heart or breathing stops, decisions about CPR should be made in advance if possible.

CPR includes external cardiac massage (pumping on the chest to keep the blood flowing through the heart) and mouth-to-mouth breathing. It may also include drugs, electric defibrillators (machines to shock the heart into action) or a breathing machine (mechanical ventilation).

CPR was originally developed for people whose hearts had stopped from a heart attack or drowning. If a healthy person's heart stops (cardiac arrest), there is a good chance of reviving the individual and returning him or her to normal life. CPR can give this person many extra years of good quality living.

In chronically ill older adults, CPR is nearly always unsuccessful. The few who do survive often do not live very long. In hospitals today, medical staff are required to do everything possible to save a person's life. Unless clear instructions are given to the contrary, every patient is given CPR.

A "No CPR" order means that no attempt should be made to revive a person whose breathing or heart has stopped. Orders like these are becoming more common as many people fear that medical technology will be used to prolong life artificially and leave them with a poor quality of life (irreversible/intolerable condition). Others just want a peaceful end to their lives and don't want to die with strangers pumping on their chests or having electric shocks in attempts to revive them.

Few people consider these decisions prior to an emergency. But people's wishes should be known in advance so that those who want CPR can receive it, and those who don't will not be subjected to it.

This Directive enables you to decide in advance about CPR. You can record your wishes in the Health and Personal Care Chart.

9

Personal Care Issues

When we become ill or confused, we need others to assist with our personal care. We may require assistance with grooming, dressing, feeding, going to the toilet, shopping or choosing where to live. The substitute decision-maker nominated in the "Let Me Decide" Advance Directive can make decisions about your personal care, if this becomes necessary. It's very important to tell your substitute your personal care wishes so this person will know what you would want and what to do. There are some issues in particular you may want to consider and discuss.

SHELTER

"Promise me that you will never put me in a home. I want to die in my own home." A parent who gets a child to make promises like this, or a

34

child who accepts this promise, is creating a recipe for trouble. Sometimes it becomes impossible to keep a parent or loved one at home. The care needed simply becomes too heavy a burden for the family.

Before you ask your family to make promises like this, consider this example. You have become so confused that you cannot wash, dress or feed yourself. You do not recognize your family members, and you have lost control of your bladder and bowels. You are wandering away all the time and become violent when your family and caregivers try to take you home again. In this condition, would you expect your family to care for you at home? People who are severely confused have no insight into their problems. Many believe they are still able to manage, even when they are very confused and unable to care for themselves.

People in this condition can place an intolerable burden on their family members and friends. Sometimes, in spite of the best intentions, it's just not possible to keep somebody like this at home.

If parents insist on staying at home with no exceptions, they set their family up for a lifetime of guilt and regret when they have no choice but to place them in a nursing home. The family feel that they have failed and let the parent down because they put them in an institution.

Don't make unreasonable demands on your caregivers and family. It's better to say, "I want to stay in my home as long as possible. Do not put me in a nursing home if you can still keep me at home. I would prefer to live six months in my own home than three years in a nursing home. Keep me at home as long as possible. Only transfer me to a nursing home if I am a danger to others or if my care becomes completely unmanageable at home. Take a reverse mortgage if you must to pay for people to come in. I will accept any reasonable risk."

Make a statement like this and avoid the word "never".

NUTRITION

Some people have special food preferences for religious or personal reasons. You can state your wishes in your Personal Statement. Please make sure to discuss your preferences with your substitute. Some people are transferred to nursing homes because they are losing weight and not eating properly at home. Many old people refuse to eat a balanced diet and seem to live on "tea and toast." Tell your substitute if you would want to be transferred to a nursing home if you were not eating a proper diet and losing weight while still at home. Other decisions about feeding are covered in the

Feeding section of the "Let Me Decide" Directive.

RESTRAINTS

Many adults who are confused are physically restrained in hospitals and nursing homes. Physical restraints include bed rails that are raised and jackets that zip up the back and are tied to beds or chairs. Other devices include chairs and tables locked together or lap belts that cannot be undone independently. Some people are even tied with wrists and ankle cuffs. In a recent survey, we found about half of the people over 75 had been physically restrained at some time in a large hospital. The main reason given for using restraints was to protect the person from falling.

Physical restraints have never been proven to protect anyone from harm; in fact, they can cause injury and even death. It is very important to discuss this issue with your substitute, because sick or confused people are often tied up in hospitals against their wishes. Here is an example of a statement that you may want to consider adding to your Personal Statement: "I don't want to be physically restrained for my own safety. Only apply physical restraints if I am a danger to others." You may want to consider whether you would prefer to wander and be at risk of falling or getting lost *or* be tied up (physical restraint) or drugged (chemical restraint) for your own safety.

On the other hand, some people in hospital or in a nursing home are very unsteady and could fall if they walk on their own. This may result in serious injuries. The hospital staff feels it must restrain these people because constant supervision can't be provided for all patients. Some people would tolerate restraints if they prevented them from falling and breaking bones.

Others who are confused may pull out intravenous tubes and interfere with medical equipment. In these situations, restraints may be considered a short-term solution if the confusion is temporary. You may wish to make a statement such as, " I would accept a physical restraint for a short time if it increased safety while I was confused."

SAFETY

Some safety issues arise at home when people have physical problems or loss of memory. They may be at risk of falls or injuries, or of fire from smoking or dangerous use of stoves. They may be at risk of wandering and getting injured or lost.

Fear for their safety often leads family members to consider moving the person to a nursing home. But there are some steps, like disconnecting the stove, providing Meals-on-Wheels or installing a personal alarm system, which reduce the risk.

In many cases it comes down to a judgment call as to how much risk family and caregivers can tolerate by keeping the person at home. A statement such as the following may be very helpful: "I will accept a risk of injury or even death to be able to stay in my own home. Only move me to a nursing home if I'm a danger to others." Another person might say, "I want to be safe and if I am not safe at home please move me to a nursing home," or, "Please move me to a nursing home if the burden becomes too great on my family."

CLOTHING AND HYGIENE

If you have preferences for clothing or headgear based on religious or personal preference, please use the Personal Statement to express them. Remember to discuss these issues with your substitute.

Many older confused people resist regular bathing and showers. If you wish, you may want to make a statement that you would only wish to be washed if your personal hygiene became offensive to others or a risk to your health.

10

The Personal Statement

Consider this part of the "Let Me Decide" Health Care Directive very carefully. The more exact you can be, the easier it will be for others to follow your wishes. Discuss this thoroughly with your substitutes, family and doctor.

People have different ideas about what disabilities and medical treatments they consider intolerable. Some would not want to be resuscitated if they were paralysed. Others fear losing bowel or bladder control. Some would not want to live in an institution, and others would not want to be tube fed. Others would not tolerate being washed and fed by others.

The Personal Statement defines what you would consider irreversible/intolerable. In this irreversible condition you would probably not want aggressive treatment to prolong your life.

It is important to state as clearly as possible what condition you would consider irreversible/intolerable. There are some simple rules that you should follow when you draft your Personal Statement.

DON'T NAME DISEASES

When you describe the condition you consider irreversible/intolerable, do not say, "if I had Alzheimer's disease or cancer." You could have skin cancer that was completely curable. Don't *name* diseases, because there are great variations in the disabilities that these diseases cause. Many people with early Alzheimer's experience only minor problems and live independently. They can shop, cook and drive. Describe what you consider irreversible in terms of everyday living.

CONSIDER "AND" AND "OR"

When you list conditions, use the words "and" and "or" carefully. This statement: "I would consider my condition irreversible/intolerable if I can't wash *and* dress *and* feed myself" is very different from   " if I can't wash *or* dress *or* feed myself." When "and" is used in the first statement, all three situations must be present, before your condition is irreversible/intolerable. If "or" is used, only one of the three must be present before your condition becomes irreversible/intolerable.

IF I HAVE LESS THAN SIX MONTHS TO LIVE

Never use a statement like "If I am terminally ill or have less than six months to live." I have met lots of people who were still alive many years after they were given six months to live. It's often very difficult to predict how long people will live with serious illnesses.

DESCRIBE EVERYDAY FUNCTIONS

"If the time ever comes when I am unable to dress myself, or recognize my family, or if I lose control over my bladder or bowel and there is no hope of recovery, then I would consider that to be an irreversible/intolerable condition." This is a good statement because any irreversible/ intolerable illness that causes permanent disability or injury and limits your independence and freedom is covered. It is better to say, "If the time ever comes when I am unable to wash, dress or feed myself" or, "If I can't speak to my family or make my wishes known and there is no hope of recovery" or, "If my family can't care for me at home and I must live in an institution."

Consider some of the following conditions when you prepare your statement.

-   chronic incurable pain

-   in permanent coma

- unable to feed, wash, dress, walk or talk
- blind, deaf
- not able to recognize family
- not able to communicate
- loss of control over bowel or bladder
- paralysed from the neck down or on one side

When you define the condition you consider irreversible or intolerable, consider what level of care you would want in that condition. If a condition is irreversible/intolerable, most people request palliative care and No CPR.

In your Personal Statement try to mention any specific wishes you might have. If you don't want certain medical procedures used under any circumstances, for religious or other reasons, say this in your statement. If you have any particular quirks about how you would like to be buried or cremated, you can also use the Personal Statement for that purpose.

Some examples of personal statements are included below for your guidance.

EXAMPLES OF PERSONAL STATEMENTS

Example No. 1
Jane is 79 years old and recently widowed. She

has no immediate family and lives alone in her own home. Although she is in good health at the moment, she realizes that this could change at any time.

Jane has told her substitute (power of attorney, proxy, mandatory) that she would consider an irreversible/intolerable condition: "A stroke or other illness that caused me to lose my speech, paralysed one side or left me permanently unable to wash, dress or feed myself." She would want *palliative* care and *basic* feeding only, no tubes or intravenous feeding, and she would want *No CPR* if she had a cardiac arrest in this condition.

However, if she got sick *now* with a reversible illness, she would like CPR if she had a cardiac arrest. If she develops a life-threatening illness she would want *surgical* care, but no ICU. She would like *supplemental* feeding if she could not eat on her own.

She wants to stay in her own home as long as possible, but she does not want to put others at risk. Jane has indicated her health care choices for an acceptable and irreversible/intolerable condition in her Health Care Chart and has discussed them with her substitute. She has also made a statement about her personal care wishes. Her Personal Statement reads as follows:

I would consider an irreversible/intolerable condition to be any condition that left me unable to wash, dress or feed myself, or that left me unable to speak. I want to stay at home as long as possible. Do not put me in a nursing home if I am not eating, washing, grooming or keeping my house clean. I can accept personal risk of wandering, falling or injuring myself, but I do not want to put others at risk. If I am putting others at risk (e.g. by causing a fire) or my care becomes too much for my friends, then I would accept going into a nursing home. I would never want to be physically restrained for my own safety.

Example No. 2

John is 64 years old and has Parkinson's disease. He is presently able to pilot his own plane with a co-pilot, and is aware that as his disease progresses he will become less active and independent. He told his substitute that he cannot accept being totally bedridden and totally dependent on others for personal care, such as washing, dressing or feeding.

He discussed his choices for acceptable and irreversible/intolerable conditions with his substitute (power of attorney, proxy, mandatory). If he is in an irreversible/intolerable condition, he would not want his life maintained by artificial means. He wants *palliative care, No CPR* and *supplemental feeding* when this time comes.

At the present time, he is in a acceptable condition, and he would want *surgical care* for a life-threatening illness, and *CPR* in the event of a cardiac arrest. He would want special diets, intravenous fluids and feeding tubes if necessary. He also made some statements about his personal care.

His Personal Statement reads as follows:

I would consider an irreversible/intolerable condition to be any condition that left me totally bedridden and totally dependent on others for personal care such as washing, dressing or feeding. I will go to a nursing home when my care becomes too difficult for my wife. I would not accept physical restraints for my safety, only to protect others. Let me eat what I ask for, even if it is not the best for my health. Don't ever force me to be bathed or groomed against my will.

Example No. 3

Nancy is a 35-year–old nurse. She has two young children. At this time she has a good quality of life and is in an acceptable condition. Now, if she developed any life-threatening illness she would want *intensive care.* If she had a cardiac arrest she would want *CPR.* Right now she wants nothing held back, and would want blood tests, IV's, x-rays and scans. She would want *supplemental feeding,* but no tube or intravenous feeding. But she would accept an intravenous for comfort – for example, if it were given to treat dehydration.

She considers an irreversible/intolerable condition to be any disease or accident that disables her to the point where she can no longer function independently. In this condition she would only want palliative care. As long as she has use of her hands and can look after herself, she would accept this. She can accept paraplegia (paralysed from the waist down). She cannot accept quadriplegia, or a stroke that significantly affected her speech, left her incontinent and she needed others to wash and dress her. In this state she would want palliative care and No CPR. She would want a painless death – peaceful and quiet – no blood work, no IV, no x-rays, no scans and no tube feeding.

She would not mind a post mortem, and would donate any organs that may be used for others.

Nancy stated her health care choices for an acceptable and an irreversible/intolerable condition in her Health Care Chart and discussed them with her substitutes. She also made a statement about her personal care. Her Personal Statement reads as follows:

I would consider an irreversible/intolerable condition to be any condition that left me unable to wash or dress myself, or that left me unable to speak, or incontinent, or that left me quadriplegic. I would not consider paraplegia "irreversible/intolerable". I would only accept a nursing home if my care became too much for my family. I would accept temporary restraints for my safety. I wish to be kept clean, I want to wear street clothes (not nightgowns) during the day. Please include me in all festivities, parties and activities if possible.

Example No. 4

Tom is a 60-year-old with chronic bronchitis. He has been in hospital three times this year already. On the last occasion he was put on a breathing machine (ventilator) because he could not breathe for himself. Now he can't walk out to pick up the mail because he gets so short of breath. He is happy now but does not want things to get much worse.

If he gets sick again, he wants antibiotics, aerosols, or oxygen by mask, but does not want to be put on the breathing machine again. His main fear is that he would not be able to get off the breathing machine and would be stuck on it. If he has a cardiac arrest, he would want No CPR. If he can't eat, he would want an *intravenous* line and *supplemental feeding*. He does not want any feeding tubes.

He would agree to a post mortem and would be glad to donate any organs that are needed to help someone else.

He has thought about this and discussed it with his substitute. His Personal Statement reads as follows:

> *I would consider an irreversible/intolerable condition to be any condition that left me unable to walk or take care of myself and had no hope of recovery. I do not want to be put on a breathing machine again. I will accept a nursing home when my wife can't cope with me at home anymore. I want to continue drinking alcohol with my meals. Please attend to my personal care, such as washing, dressing and grooming. I would not accept physical restraints except to protect others.*

Example No. 5

Bob is a 65-year-old retired executive. He used to love golf and fishing. Four years ago he had a heart attack and last year he had bypass surgery. Now he has angina when he climbs stairs, and sometimes wakes up short of breath.

Last time he was in hospital, he had a cardiac arrest and had to be brought back. He knows that he could go at any second. Should he have another heart attack he would not want to be resuscitated, and he does not want any more surgery. If he goes into failure again he would want *limited care* with *supplemental feeding,* but does not want to go into the intensive care unit. He does not want intravenous feeding. He does not want any feeding tubes passed into his stomach if he ever became unconscious or unable to eat.

He would not mind a post mortem and would be happy to give his organs to anyone who needed them.

After filling out his Health Care Chart and discussing his wishes with his substitute, Bob completed his Personal Statement as follows:

I would consider an irreversible/intolerable condition to be any condition that left me unable to walk, dress or take care of myself. I would accept a nursing home if my care becomes too difficult for my wife and family, I'm a strict vegetarian and I don't want any meat or fish. But continue to give me lots of fresh fruit, vegetables and chocolate. I would accept physical restraints for my own and others' safety.

Example No. 6

Jason is a 35-year-old patient with AIDS. He has been in the hospital three times this year and has lost fifty pounds since his illness began. When he becomes ill again he wants intravenous antibiotics, but he does not want intensive care. He does not want any intravenous feeding or feeding tubes and he does not want a breathing machine (ventilator). If he has a cardiac arrest, he does not want CPR. He does not want to die with people pumping his chest.

Having discussed his wishes with his substitutes and completed his Health Care Chart, Jason wrote his Personal Statement as follows:

> *I would consider an irreversible/intolerable condition to be any condition that left me permanently confined to bed or that caused me to spend most of my time in hospital. Thank you for all your care – I deeply appreciate it. Do everything to avoid hospitalization. I would want to die at home if at all possible. Never restrain me physically for any reason, unless I am a danger to others. Keep me comfortable. Grooming, dressing and feeding are secondary.*

ORGAN DONATION

In the last twenty years, since drugs have been developed to prevent the body's rejection of transplanted tissue from other humans, organ donation has become widespread. Many of us know someone who is alive today only because he or she received a heart, lung, kidney, liver or bone-marrow transplant from another. Some people who were blind can see again because of corneal transplants.

A section on blood transfusion has been included for Jehovah's Witnesses. There is also a section for cremation and a post mortem.

11

Filling Out the Directive

It is an important decision to use the "Let Me Decide" Health and Personal Care Directive. Take your time, think about what you want and follow these steps.

SUBSTITUTES

Choose at least one family member or friend who will complete the document with you. Select someone you trust to understand your wishes and respect your position in this matter. This person will become your *substitute* (power of attorney, proxy, mandatory). You can name more than one person as your substitute (power of attorney, proxy or mandatory).

AUTHORITY OF SUBSTITUTES

You give the substitute authority to make decisions about any health and personal care area if you are mentally incapable of making decisions for yourself. This document does not allow your substitute to make decisions about your property or finances. You need to complete a separate form for this. You can assign different powers to different individuals. There is no overlap.

MAKE SURE YOU UNDERSTAND

Read the document carefully. If you do not understand all the terms, read the applicable parts of the booklet again, or get more information from your family doctor or another health care professional.

WITH WHOM SHOULD I DISCUSS MY DIRECTIVE

Discuss the Directive with all those concerned before deciding to use it. Talk to your family, close friends and your doctor. But make sure the final decision is *yours,* and not the result of pressure from others. If your doctor disagrees with your decision, you may want to get a second opinion. You do not need a lawyer to complete this document. But you may want to let your lawyer know you have a Health and Personal Care Directive when you are making out or updating a property will. You do not have to complete your Advance Directive with your doctor, but it's a good idea to include your doctor because he or she may be involved when you get sick. Your doctor is knowledgeable about health care and personal care issues and should be able to answer your questions.

HOW SHALL I STORE IT?

Leave a copy with your doctor and your substitute(s). You can get a plastic wallet-sized card if you write to the address on the *back page* of the booklet. Get photocopies and share them with your lawyer and family if you wish.

JOINTLY AND SEVERALLY

(i.e. together and separately)

This phrase is only used if you have named more than one substitute. The law requires them to make decisions together, unless you give them permission to act independently or separately. If you want your substitutes to have this authority separately, leave the words "jointly and severally." But if you want them to make decisions together, delete the word "severally" and leave the word "jointly." "Jointly" means that if one is not available, decisions cannot be made on your behalf. On the other hand, it may be comforting to some to know that two people must agree on any decision on your behalf.

Go to your family doctor with your substitute. Sign the Directive and have the doctor, substitute and two witnesses co-sign it. Leave a copy of the completed form with your doctor and substitute(s).

Tell your family and friends that you have prepared this Directive, and who your substitute is. You may even want to let them have photocopies of this document.

WHAT IF I CHANGE MY MIND?

Tell your substitutes and doctor. Update all the copies of the Advance Directive. It's a good idea to update it every few years anyway. If you update and make no changes, just date and initial it with your doctor and substitutes.

REVOKING THE HEALTH AND PERSONAL CARE DIRECTIVE

To revoke this document, write down the revocation on paper, sign and date it, and have witnesses sign also. Notify your substitutes and all those who were involved in the original document.

UPDATING THE DIRECTIVE

Decide how often you would like to review this document. For example, you may decide to do this once a year, or after any illness or change in your health. This decision will depend on your age, the condition of your health, and life plans.

A completed Health Care Directive is provided for your consideration.

Glossary of Terms

AIDS: Acquired Immune Deficiency Syndrome has been strongly linked to the Human Immunodeficiency Virus (HIV), which weakens the body's defence against disease.   It is transmitted by the exchange of certain specific body fluids under specific circumstances, and not by casual contact. There is no known cure.

ALZHEIMER'S DISEASE: A disease of the brain causing progressive memory loss.   With time, there is loss of ability to learn and, eventually, loss of the ability to do even simple tasks. The patient's behaviour may also change. There is no known cure.

ANAESTHETIC: A local anaesthetic "freezes" the skin by making it numb to pain. With general anaesthetic, a person is temporarily "put to sleep": this is used only for major medical procedures.

ANGINA OR ANGINA PECTORIS: Chest pain due to poor blood-flow to the heart, which usually occurs with exercise, and goes away with rest. The pain may spread to the arms and/or neck. This means that the blood supply to the heart is inadequate. If it persists, the heart muscle may be damaged and result in a heart attack.

ANTIBIOTICS: Drugs used to treat infections caused by bacteria.

BASIC LIFE SUPPORT: Mouth-to-mouth resuscitation and heart massage (see **CPR,** below).

BIOPSY: Surgical removal of tissue so that it may be examined under a microscope for evidence of disease.

BRONCHOSCOPY: A procedure in which the physician looks through a flexible tube into the airways of the lungs, using a scope with a light on the tip.

BYPASS SURGERY: Replacement or re-routing of blood vessels to an area of the body where the blood flow is not adequate.

CARDIAC ARREST: Stoppage of heartbeat.

CHF: Congestive Heart Failure, caused by failure of the heart to maintain adequate circulation of blood, resulting in weakness and shortness of breath.

COLONOSCOPY: A procedure in which a physician looks into the large bowel through a flexible tube known as a scope.

CORNEA: The clear, front surface of the eye.

CORNEAL TRANSPLANT: Surgical replacement of a damaged cornea with a donated cornea.

COPD: Chronic Obstructive Pulmonary Disease, caused by problems in the airways leading to the lungs or in the lungs themselves. The main symptom is chronic shortness of breath.

CPR: Cardio-Pulmonary Resuscitation, the use of mouth-to-mouth breathing and heart massage to restore heartbeat.

CT: Computerized Tomography or CAT scan, use of a computer to produce, from x-ray data, a view of part of the body.

CYSTIC FIBROSIS: An inherited disease that causes chronic lung infections and poor function of the pancreas in young people. There is no known cure, but treatment can prolong the patient's life to about 30 years of age.

DEFIBRILLATOR: An instrument that shocks the heart with an electric current to revive it or to correct its rhythm.

DEHYDRATION: Loss of water from the body.

DIALYSIS: A method of filtering and cleaning the blood of patients with kidney problems.

ECT: Electroconvulsive therapy, the use of an electric shock to treat specific types of mental illness, for example, acute depression.

EEG: Electroencephalogram, a method of measuring brain activity.

EMG: Electromyogram, a method of measuring muscle and nerve function.

ENDOSCOPY: Looking inside any body cavity by means of a scope.

EXTERNAL CARDIAC MASSAGE: Massage of the heart by applying pressure on the chest to maintain circulation.

FIBRE-OPTIC SCOPE: An instrument used for looking inside body cavities.

FRACTURED HIP: A break in the thigh bone (the femur) between the hip and the knee. Breaks usually occur at the upper part of the femur just below the hip bone (the pelvis).

GASTROSTOMY: A surgical opening make so that a tube can be put directly into the stomach, usually for feeding.

HEPATITIS: Swelling of the liver, caused by alcohol abuse, viral, or bacterial infections.

INCONTINENCE: Loss of control of bladder or bowel.

INTESTINE: Bowel.

INTOLERABLE/UNACCEPTABLE:
Disability that is associated with such a poor quality of life that the person would not want

technology used to prolong life. At this stage the person would just want palliative care for life threatening illness and no CPR in the event of cardiac arrest.

INTRAVENOUS (IV): Injection of fluid into the body through a fine tube into a vein.

INVESTIGATIONS: Tests done by the doctor, such as blood tests, scans, x-rays, etc.

IRREVERSIBLE ILLNESS: An illness that cannot be cured.

KIDNEY MACHINE: The machine used in dialysis to clean the blood of people with kidney problems.

LAPAROTOMY: Surgery to explore the abdomen, usually to find the cause of pain or blockage.

LIFE SUPPORT: Machines used to keep a person alive by maintaining circulation and ventilation (breathing).

LIFE-THREATENING ILLNESS: Any illness that can cause death.

NASOGASTRIC TUBE: Tube put down the nose and into the stomach for feeding or drainage.

PALLIATIVE CARE: Care that provides comfort and relief from pain, but does not aim to cure a condition.

PARAPLEGIA: Loss of all sensation and movement in the lower half of the body.

PERSONAL STATEMENT: Section in the "Let Me Decide" Directive where people state what level of irreversible disability they consider unacceptable, and express their wishes regarding levels of care, post mortem, organ donation, blood transfusion, and cremation or burial.

PNEUMONIA: Infection and congestion of the lungs.

POST MORTEM: Autopsy, usually to find the cause of death.

PULMONARY EMBOLISM: Blood clot in the lung that often arises or breaks off from a clot in the calves.

QUADRIPLEGIA: Loss of all sensation and movement below the neck.

RESUSCITATE: To restore life by giving mouth-to-mouth breathing and/or heart massage.

REVERSIBLE ILLNESS: An illness that can be cured.

SCAN: A method of looking inside the body without surgery. Can involve the injection of a dye that can be seen by a special x-ray.

SLE: Systemic Lupus Erythematosus (Lupus), a chronic disease that affects many organs, joints and skin. It is caused when the body's defence mechanism turns on itself. The course of the disease varies greatly from person to person; however, it is not curable.

SPECIAL DIET: Diet geared to the specific nutritional needs of patients such as diabetics.

STROKE: Sudden damage to the brain caused by lack of oxygen, often resulting in weakness, slurred speech, loss of movement, etc. These losses may or may not improve over time.

TERMINAL ILLNESS: Illness from which a person will not recover and will eventually die.

TIA: Transient Ischemic Attack, temporary block of the blood supply to the brain, causing weakness, slurred speech, loss of movement and memory lapses, lasting from a few moments to several hours.

TOTAL PARENTERAL NUTRITION: Complete nutrition (proteins, sugars, fats, vitamins and minerals) given by injection through a vein.

TRANSPLANT: An organ or tissue taken from the body for use in another area of the same body or for use in another person's body.

VENTILATOR: Breathing machine or respirator.

Completed sample directive

1. INTRODUCTION

I, _____Jonathan Smith_____,
revoke any previous power of attorney for personal and health
care made by me and APPOINT: _Joan Smith,_
Margaret Brown
jointly and severally to act as my power of attorney (proxy,
mandatory) and to do on my behalf anything that I can lawfully
do by an attorney for personal care, including giving consent to
treatment. If he/she/they is/are unable, unwilling or in the event
of resignation, death, mental incapacity, refusal, or court
removal, then I appoint as alternate _David Martin_

substitute(s), power of attorney(s) (proxies, mandatories) to act
jointly and severally as my substitute(s) or attorney(s) for personal care.

[If you've named more than one substitute, (attorney, proxy
or mandatory) or more than one alternate and you want each
of them to have the authority to act separately, leave the words
"jointly or severally." If you want them to act together, not
independently, delete "and severally" and leave "jointly." If
you have named one person, delete "jointly and severally."]

Dated and signed this _15TH_ day of _FEBRUARY_ 19 _95_

G. Smith   _Jonathan Smith_   _0000 925 836_
Signature   Print Name   Health Card No.

2. PERSONAL CARE

I would consider an irreversible/intolerable condition to be any condition

IF I WAS UNABLE TO COMMUNICATE
MY NEEDS OR I DID NOT RECOGNIZE MY
FAMILY; IF I WAS TOTALLY DEPENDENT
FOR BATHING, DRESSING, GROOMING OR
TOILET; IF I WAS IN CONSTANT PAIN.
I WOULD ACCEPT MOVING TO A NURSING
HOME IF MY FAMILY COULD NOT COPE
WITH MY CARE ANYMORE.
I WOULD NOT ACCEPT PHYSICAL
RESTRAINTS FOR MY OWN SAFETY --
ONLY FOR THE SAFETY OF OTHERS.

I would agree to the following procedures: (write YES or NO)

Blood Transfusion __YES__   Post Mortem __YES__

Organ Donation __YES__   Cremation __YES__

3. THE HEALTH CARE CHART

(opposite page)

	If my condition is Acceptable				If my condition is Irreversible/Intolerable		
	Life-Threatening Illness	Cardiac Arrest	Feeding		Life-Threatening Illness	Cardiac Arrest	Feeding
	Palliative Limited Surgical Intensive	No CPR CPR	Basic Supplemental Intravenous Tube		Palliative Limited Surgical Intensive	No CPR CPR	Basic Supplemental Intravenous Tube
	INTENSIVE	CPR	TUBE		PALLIATIVE	NO CPR	BASIC

Date Feb 15, 1995 Signature *J Smith* Power of Attorney Signature(s) *Marion Jean Smith* Physician Signature *(signed)*

Update once a year, after an illness, or if there is any change in health

NO CHANGE

Date March 1, 1996 Signature *J Smith* Power of Attorney Signature(s) Physician Signature *(signed)*

Date Signature Power of Attorney Signature(s) Physician Signature

5. SIGNATURES

Family Physician

Name: DR. JANE TUTTLE

Address: 640 SPADINA ROAD

Tel: (H) 222-4522   Tel: (W) 921-8882

Signature: Jane Tuttle

Power of Attorney(s)/Substitute(s)/ Proxy(s)

1. Name: MARGARET BROWN

Tel: (H) 391-5397   Tel: (W) 585-9191

Mobile Tel: _____

Address: 1568 PARKLANE AVE

2. Name: JOAN SMITH

Tel: (H) 471-8927   Tel: (W) 395-4871

Mobile Tel: _____

Address: 73 JUNIPER DRIVE, WILLOWDALE
M4V 3T6

Witnesses

1. Name: B.L. ALLEN

Address: 10 ALCORN AVE, TORONTO, ONT

Tel: (H) (416) 555-1212   Tel: (W) (416) 666-1122

Signature: B Allen

2. Name: Brian Higginbottom

Address: 35 Sheldrake Blvd., Toronto, Ont.
M4G 1V8

Tel: (H) (416) 422-2913   Tel: (W) _____

Signature: B Higginbottom .

NEWGRANGE PRESS

Website: www.newgrangepress.com

PUBLICATIONS

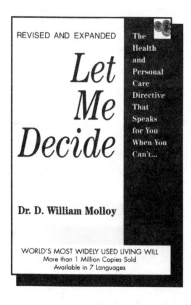

REVISED AND EXPANDED

Let Me Decide

The Health and Personal Care Directive That Speaks for You When You Can't...

Dr. D. William Molloy

WORLD'S MOST WIDELY USED LIVING WILL
More than 1 Million Copies Sold
Available in 7 Languages

THE LET ME DECIDE PROGRAM

Through age, illness or accident, people may lose their capacity to understand the nature and consequences of proposed health and personal care decisions. These decisions then fall to families, friends and physicians who may not be aware of the patient's wishes and intent. The health care directive contained in this booklet lets you plan your own future health and personal care in advance. It makes sure your wishes will be known, when you no longer can understand your options or communicate your choices to others. Developed over many years of research and consultation, the Let Me Decide health and personal care directive

cont. inside

- Gives each individual the opportunity to choose different levels of treatment according to his or her wishes.
- Helps relieve family and friends of responsibility for decisions in a time of crisis.
- Guides health care practitioners in making vital decisions when family members are unavailable.
- Has received enthusiastic support from a wide variety of individuals and groups including doctors, patients, social workers, lawyers, clergy and advocates for the elderly and the disabled.

Let Me Decide is available in French, German, Italian, Japanese, Spanish and Swedish. Let Me Decide is a complete health care program with three videos in English and French.

1) My Health Care - I Decide
2) My Health Care - Understanding My Choices
3) My Health Care - Filling out the Directive
"Train the Trainer" Workshops and lectures are available on request.

LET ME PASS GENTLY

This is a comprehensive guide to the "Let Me Decide" Advance Directive Program. This book describes the legal, clinical, ethical, spiritual, social and economic issues with the use of implementation of the "Let Me Decide" program in different settings and different countries. It contains a wealth of information about advance directives and the "Let Me Decide" program. "Let Me Pass Gently" provides the instruments developed for the program, policies, case histories, terminology and over twenty-five publications on "Let Me Decide".
-release date Summer 2000.

CAPACITY TO DECIDE
Dr. D. W. Molloy,
Dr. P. Darzins, Dr. Strang

Capacity to Decide is a short, comprehensive book which describes a new six step capacity assessment that measures decision-specific capacity, with clear instructions on its use. This book describes how this new assessment process can be applied to measure capacity for:

- personal care
- health care
- property and finances
- advance directives
- Wills and Power of Attorney
- driving
- sexuality and intimacy

"Capacity to Decide" is a practical guide and invaluable tool for health care workers, members of the legal profession and anyone who needs to measure capacity in patients or clients.

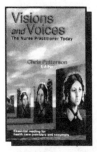

VISIONS AND VOICES... THE NURSE PRACTITIONER TODAY
Christine Patterson (Editor)

Visions and Voices: The Nurse Practitioner Today is a comprehensive overview of the political, economic and social factors that influence advanced practice role of nurses. In this book, contributors from different organizations outline the political process, educational challenges and legal implications of advance practice. Nurse practitioners discuss their roles and the problems faced in role development. Physicians relate their experiences working with nurse practitioners in different primary, secondary and tertiary care settings. This book is a unique, detailed account of the challenges faced by professional nursing as it redefines its role in health care.

NURSE PRACTITIONERS...
THE CATALYST OF CHANGE
Christine Patterson (Editor)

A new nurse practitioner book, complementary to Visions and Voices. Both books are timely and make a significant contribution to outlining how nursing organized itself to realize a vision.

STANDARDIZED
MINI MENTAL
STATE EXAMINATION
Dr. D. W. Molloy

The Folstein mini-mental state examination (MMSE) is the most widely used screening test of cognition in older adults. The Standardized Mini-Mental State Examination (SMMSE) provides clear, explicit administration and scoring guidelines.

The SMMSE can be used in the diagnosis and treatment of dementia. It is used to stage the disease, differentiate between the different dementias and assess response to treatment.

STANDARDIZED MINI-MENTAL
STATE EXAMINATION:
A USERS GUIDE
Dr. D. W. Molloy and Dr. Roger Clarnette

This short booklet contains a standardized version of the Standardized Mini-Mental State Examination (SMMSE) and describes how this short test can be used to diagnose and treat cognitive impairment in older adults. The book describes how the SMMSE is used to stage dementia, assess treatment and develop care plans.

The pattern changes on the SMMSE provide valuable clues to the cause of cognitive impairment. This short booklet is packed with practical clinical tips,diagnostic aids, tables and figures.

HOW DO YOU SAY?
(Italian Version
Com Si Dice)
*Dr. D.W. Molloy and
Dr. S. Salama.*

Practical, user-friendly communication aid for health care workers and Italian patients. Contains sections on general conversation, personal needs, medical terms, pictionary and dictionary.

FOR MORE INFORMATION OR TO ORDER

Newgrange Press (Canada)
428 Orkney Road, RR1 Troy, Ontario, Canada L0R 2B0
Tel: (905) 628-0354 Fax: (905) 628-4901
E-mail: idecide@netcom.ca
Website: www.newgrangepress.com

Newgrange Press (U.S.A.)
301 Highland Avenue
Winchester, MA 01890
telephone/fax: 781.729.8981
E-mail: jamesmcinerny@hotmail.com

Newgrange Press (Ireland)
The Stables, Woodstown, Waterford, Ireland
Tel: 353-51-870152 Fax: 353-51-871214

Newgrange Press (Australia)
P.O. Box 7077 Shenton Park, W. Australia 6008
Tel: 61-8-93896433 Fax: 61-8-93896455
E-mail: clarnett@medeserv.com.au

Newgrange Press (Japan)
100-1, Kashiyama, Habikino, Osaka (583-0886) Japan
Tel: 81729-542000 Fax: 81-729-547560

Newgrange Press (Austria)
Willersdorferstrasse 6
A-8061 St. Radegund Austria
Tel: 0043-3132-3472 Fax: 0043-3132-3472-15

NEWGRANGE PRESS ORDER FORM

Let Me Decide (LMD) Booklets	Price	Qty	Total
English	$10.00		
French	$10.00		
German	$15.00		
Italian	$10.00		
Japanese	$15.00		
Spanish	$10.00		
Swedish	$15.00		
LMD Audio Tape/ Talking Book	$15.00		
LMD Single Videos (English ○ French ○)			
My Health Care - I Decide	$30.00		
My Health Care - Understanding My Choices	$30.00		
My Health Care - Filling out the Directive	$30.00		
Video Series (set of 3)(English ○ French ○)	$90.00		
LMD Bulk/Directive/Forms			
Personal	$1.00 ea		
Next-of-Kin	$1.00 ea		
LMD "The Works" complete package includes:	$150.00		
3 Videos (English ○ French ○)			
1 Set of Slides			
1 Let Me Decide Book			
(English, French, German, Spanish, Italian)			
Research Publications			
Training Manual	$39.95		
Capacity to Decide	$24.00		
How Do You Say? (Italian ver. Com Si Dice)	$10.00		
Standardized Mini Mental State Exam. (SMMSE)	$5.00		
SMMSE User's Guide	$10.00		
Visions and Voices...The Nurse Practitioner Today	$20.00		
Nurse Practitioners...The Catalyst of Change	$24.00		
Let Me Pass Gently	$29.95		
Set Me Free	$10.00		
Total of Order			
Please add 7% GST on Canadian orders and sales tax where applicable on US order			
Postage & Handling, 15% (or minimum of $2.50) on total order only			
GRAND TOTAL:			

Payment can be made by cheque or money order Payable to "Newgrange Press".
Books will be mailed within 7 days of payment.